1950 U.K. YEARBOOK

ISBN: 9781098683856

This book gives a fascinating and informative insight into life in the United Kingdom in 1950. It includes everything from the most popular music of the year to the cost of a buying a new house. Additionally, there are chapters covering people in high office, the best-selling films of the year and all the main news and events. Want to know which team won the FA Cup or which British personalities were born in 1950? All this and much more awaits you within.

© Liberty Eagle Publishing Ltd. 2019
All Rights Reserved

INDEX

	Page
Calendar	4
People In High Office	5
British News & Events	9
Worldwide News & Events	16
Births - UK Personalities	20
Notable British Deaths	26
Popular Music	28
Top 5 Films	34
Sporting Winners	50
Cost Of Living	57

FIRST EDITION

1950

January
M	T	W	T	F	S	S
						1
2	3	4	5	6	7	8
9	10	11	12	13	14	15
16	17	18	19	20	21	22
23	24	25	26	27	28	29
30	31					

◐:4 ●:11 ◑:18 ○:26

February
M	T	W	T	F	S	S
		1	2	3	4	5
6	7	8	9	10	11	12
13	14	15	16	17	18	19
20	21	22	23	24	25	26
27	28					

◐:2 ◑:9 ●:16 ○:25

March
M	T	W	T	F	S	S
		1	2	3	4	5
6	7	8	9	10	11	12
13	14	15	16	17	18	19
20	21	22	23	24	25	26
27	28	29	30	31		

○:4 ◑:11 ●:18 ◐:26

April
M	T	W	T	F	S	S
					1	2
3	4	5	6	7	8	9
10	11	12	13	14	15	16
17	18	19	20	21	22	23
24	25	26	27	28	29	30

○:2 ◑:9 ●:17 ◐:25

May
M	T	W	T	F	S	S
1	2	3	4	5	6	7
8	9	10	11	12	13	14
15	16	17	18	19	20	21
22	23	24	25	26	27	28
29	30	31				

◐:2 ◑:8 ●:17 ◐:24 ○:31

June
M	T	W	T	F	S	S
			1	2	3	4
5	6	7	8	9	10	11
12	13	14	15	16	17	18
19	20	21	22	23	24	25
26	27	28	29	30		

◑:7 ●:15 ◐:23 ○:29

July
M	T	W	T	F	S	S
					1	2
3	4	5	6	7	8	9
10	11	12	13	14	15	16
17	18	19	20	21	22	23
24	25	26	27	28	29	30
31						

◑:7 ●:15 ◐:22 ○:29

August
M	T	W	T	F	S	S
	1	2	3	4	5	6
7	8	9	10	11	12	13
14	15	16	17	18	19	20
21	22	23	24	25	26	27
28	29	30	31			

◑:5 ●:13 ◐:20 ○:27

September
M	T	W	T	F	S	S
				1	2	3
4	5	6	7	8	9	10
11	12	13	14	15	16	17
18	19	20	21	22	23	24
25	26	27	28	29	30	

◑:4 ●:12 ◐:18 ○:26

October
M	T	W	T	F	S	S
						1
2	3	4	5	6	7	8
9	10	11	12	13	14	15
16	17	18	19	20	21	22
23	24	25	26	27	28	29
30	31					

◐:4 ●:11 ◑:18 ○:25

November
M	T	W	T	F	S	S
		1	2	3	4	5
6	7	8	9	10	11	12
13	14	15	16	17	18	19
20	21	22	23	24	25	26
27	28	29	30			

◐:3 ●:9 ◑:16 ○:24

December
M	T	W	T	F	S	S
				1	2	3
4	5	6	7	8	9	10
11	12	13	14	15	16	17
18	19	20	21	22	23	24
25	26	27	28	29	30	31

◐:2 ●:9 ◑:16 ○:24

People in High Office

Monarch - King George VI
Reign: 11th December 1936 - 6th February 1952
Predecessor: Edward VIII
Successor: Elizabeth II

United Kingdom

Clement Attlee
Prime Minister - Labour Party
26th July 1945 - 26th October 1951

Australia	Canada	United States

Prime Minister
Sir Robert Menzies
Liberal (Coalition)
19th December 1949
- 26th January 1966

Prime Minister
Louis St. Laurent
Liberal Party
15th November 1948
- 21st June 1957

President
Harry S. Truman
Democratic Party
12th April 1945
- 20th January 1953

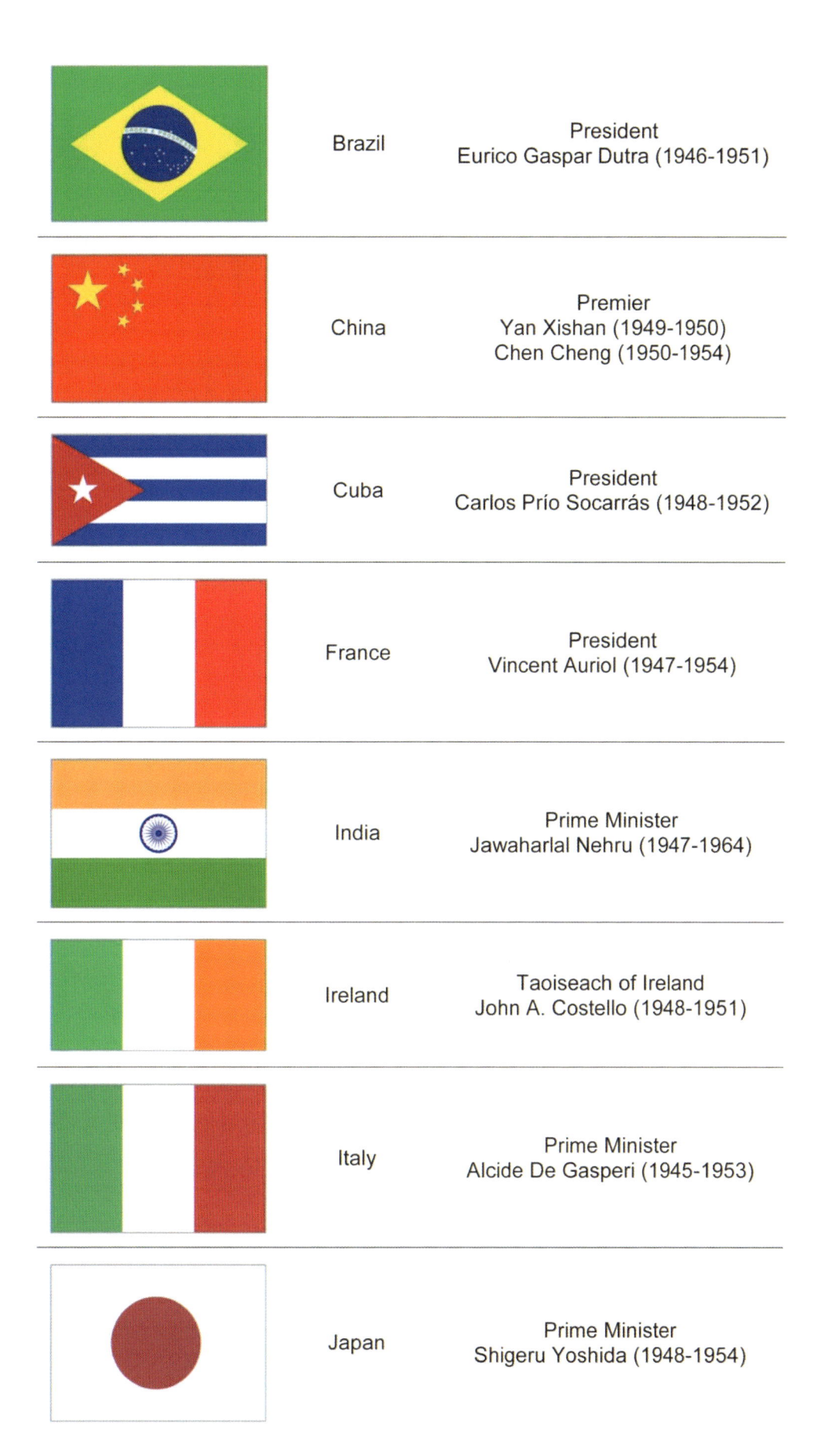

	Brazil	President Eurico Gaspar Dutra (1946-1951)
	China	Premier Yan Xishan (1949-1950) Chen Cheng (1950-1954)
	Cuba	President Carlos Prío Socarrás (1948-1952)
	France	President Vincent Auriol (1947-1954)
	India	Prime Minister Jawaharlal Nehru (1947-1964)
	Ireland	Taoiseach of Ireland John A. Costello (1948-1951)
	Italy	Prime Minister Alcide De Gasperi (1945-1953)
	Japan	Prime Minister Shigeru Yoshida (1948-1954)

	Mexico	President Miguel Alemán Valdés (1946-1952)
	New Zealand	Prime Minister Sidney Holland (1949-1957)
	Pakistan	Prime Minister Liaquat Ali Khan (1947-1951)
	Spain	President Francisco Franco (1938-1973)
	South Africa	Prime Minister Daniel François Malan (1948-1954)
	Soviet Union	Communist Party Leader Joseph Stalin (1922-1953)
	Turkey	Prime Minister Şemsettin Günaltay (1949-1950) Adnan Menderes (1950-1960)
	West Germany	Chancellor Konrad Adenauer (1949-1963)

BRITISH NEWS & EVENTS

JAN

12th | Submarine HMS Truculent collides with the Swedish oil tanker Divina in the Thames Estuary and sinks; 64 men die as a result of the collision.

16th | The BBC Light Programme first broadcasts the daily children's radio feature Listen with Mother. The programme would run until the 1st October 1982 and at its peak it had an audience of over a million listeners.

26th | Donald Hume is sentenced to imprisonment as an accessory to the murder of Stanley Setty, having dumped his dismembered body over the English Channel from a light aircraft. Hume had carried out the murder because Setty had kicked his beloved dog Tony.

FEB

4th | The 4th British Empire Games (now called the Commonwealth Games) opens in Auckland, New Zealand. The games were originally awarded to Montreal in Canada, and due to be held in 1942, but had to cancelled because of WW2.

8th | George Kelly is sentenced to hang for the double murder of the manager and assistant manager of the Cameo cinema in the Liverpool suburb of Wavertree. Despite having a sound alibi, and his continued protestations of innocence, he was executed on the 28th March 1950. *Follow up: In June 2003 Kelly's conviction was judged unsafe and was duly quashed. His remains were taken from their burial place in Walton prison by his family and he was given a dignified funeral after a service in Liverpool Metropolitan Cathedral.*

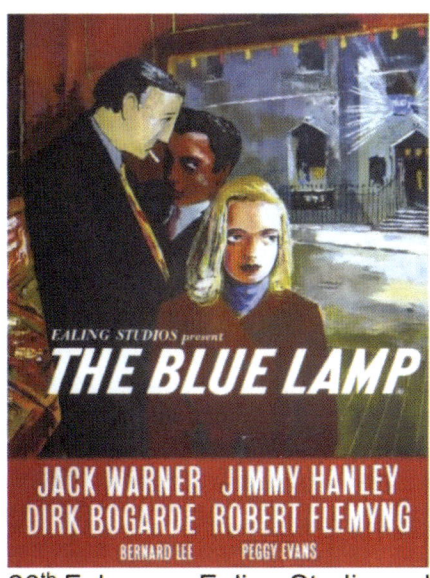

20th February: Ealing Studios release the film The Blue Lamp, introducing the character PC George Dixon, played by Jack Warner. The film became the inspiration for the TV series Dixon of Dock Green (1955-1976) where Jack Warner, pictured left in photo 2, continued to play PC Dixon until he was 80 years old (even though Dixon's murder is the central plot of the original film).

FEB

The British ocean liner RMS Aquitania on her maiden voyage in New York (1914).

21st February: The Cunard liner RMS Aquitania arrives at the scrapyard in Faslane, Scotland after having been sold to the British Iron & Steel Corporation Ltd for £125,000. The scrapping took almost a year to complete and ended an illustrious career which included steaming 3 million miles on 450 voyages. Aquitania had carried 1.2 million passengers over a career that spanned nearly 36 years, making her the longest-serving Express Liner of the 20th century and the only major liner to serve in both World Wars.

| 24th | Clement Attlee's Labour Party wins the general election giving them a second term in government, after their election triumph five years earlier in 1945. However, they retain power with a majority of just five seats, a stark contrast to the 146-seat majority that they gained previously. Among the lost Labour seats is Bexley in Kent which is won by the 33-year-old Conservative Party candidate Edward Heath from Ashley Bramall. Voter turnout is 83.9%, an all-time high for a UK general election under universal suffrage. |

MAR

| 1st | The German-born theoretical physicist Klaus Fuchs, working at Harwell Atomic Energy Research Establishment, is convicted (following a confession) of supplying secret information about the atomic bomb to the Soviet Union. He is sentenced to fourteen years imprisonment but is released in 1959 after serving just nine years and four months (at the time long-term prisoners were entitled by law to one-third off their sentence for good behaviour). |
| 6th | The World Figure Skating Championships are held at Wembley in north west London. The UK win two silver medals; Jeannette Altwegg in the ladies' competition, and Jennifer and John Nicks in the pairs. |

MAR

8th March: Carmaker Rover unveils the JET1, a revolutionary new turbine-powered concept car. It could do zero to 60mph in 14 seconds, had a maximum speed of 90 mph, and could run on petrol, paraffin or diesel. A series of prototypes were made into the 1960s but further development was dropped due too many issues in making the engines feasible for use in passenger cars. *Fun facts: Improved and modified to a more aerodynamic style in 1952, it achieved the world record for a gas turbine powered car when it reached a speed of 152.691mph.*

12th	Eighty of the eighty-three passengers on board an Avro Tudor V aircraft are killed when it stalls and crashes on its approach to land at Llandow in Glamorgan. It had been privately hired to fly rugby union enthusiasts to and from an international game in Ireland. At the time this was the world's worst air disaster.
16th	The Gambols comic strip, created by Barry Appleby, first appears in the Daily Express. It ran for almost 50 years in the Express and, as of 1999, has appeared in the Mail on Sunday.

APR

1st	Corby, a village in Northamptonshire with a population of 18,000, is designated a New Town with William Holford as its architect. By 1951 he prepared the development plan with a car-friendly layout and many areas of open space and woodland. In 1952 Holford produced the town centre plan and in 1954 the layout for the first 500 houses.
14th	The first issue of the Eagle comic is published and is an immediate success selling 900,000 copies. Featured in colour on the front cover was its most recognisable story, Dan Dare, Pilot of the Future, created by Frank Hampson with meticulous attention to detail. Other popular stories included Riders of the Range and P.C. 49.

APR

29th | Arsenal win the FA Cup with a 2-0 win over Liverpool at Wembley Stadium.

MAY

13th | The first Formula One motor race of seven in the 1950 World Championship of Drivers is held at Silverstone. The race is won by Italian driver Giuseppe Farina.

20th | Vladimir Raitz of Horizon Holidays arranges the first package holiday air charter from Gatwick Airport to Calvi, Corsica.

21st | A tornado tracks across England from Wendover to Blakeney, Norfolk. At 66 miles long it remains the longest trail on record for a tornado in England, and at two and a half hours the tornado is the longest lasting on record in Europe.

26th | Motor fuel rationing eventually comes to an end after it was introduced in the wake of the Second World War eleven years earlier.

JUN

6th June: The BBC Light Programme first broadcasts the popular radio comedy feature Educating Archie. The programme featured ventriloquist Peter Brough and his doll Archie Andrews, and proved extremely popular despite its unlikely central premise of a ventriloquist act on radio. The show introduced a number of comedians as Archie's tutor, who would all go on to be well known, including Tony Hancock, Benny Hill, Harry Secombe, Dick Emery, Bernard Bresslaw, Hattie Jacques and Bruce Forsyth. During its nearly ten year run Educating Archie averaged 15 million listeners and had a fan club boasting some 250,000 members.

22nd | The film Treasure Island, made on location at Denham Film Studios, Buckinghamshire, premieres in London. Starring Robert Newton as Long John Silver it is notable for being Disney's first completely live-action film.

JUN

24th — The fourth World Cup opens in Brazil, the first since 1938. Qualifiers Scotland withdrew from the competition before it started and England failed to get past the group stage. Uruguay were crowned champions in the final round.

29th — The first of five pilot episodes of the series The Archers is broadcast on BBC Radio. To date it has aired over 18,800 episodes and is the world's longest-running radio drama.

JUL

11th — BBC television broadcasts the first episode of the popular pre-school children's programme Andy Pandy.

31st July: Sainsbury's opens its first purpose-built self-service supermarket in Croydon. The new format, which was inspired by American food stores, was greeted with a mixed reception by 1950s shoppers used to ordering their food from counters where it would be packaged by a member of staff.

31st — In cricket Warwickshire's Eric Hollies beats Nobby Clark's record of 65 innings without reaching double figures when he is dismissed for 7 against Worcestershire. Hollies will eventually make it 71 innings before scoring 14 against Nottinghamshire on the 16th August.

AUG

8th — Florence Chadwick swims the English Channel and reaches Dover in a record time of 13 hours and 23 minutes.

15th — Princess Elizabeth gives birth to her only daughter. The new baby is third in line to the throne after her mother and older brother Charles.

19th — The Football League season begins with four new teams, taking membership from 88 to 92 across the four divisions. The new clubs are Colchester United, Gillingham, Scunthorpe United and Shrewsbury Town.

24th — Vale Park football stadium opens in Stoke-on-Trent to serve Port Vale F.C. Initially billed as the 'Wembley of the North' it cost £50,000 to build and had a capacity of 40,000 (360 seated).

AUG

29th	A British force of about 4,000 infantry arrives in Korea from Hong Kong. The force includes soldiers from the 1st Battalion of the Argyll and Sutherland Highlanders, and the 1st Battalion of the Middlesex Regiment. They were sent as back up for the American-led United Nations force - until now the only British support had been from warships in the area and some local air squadrons. *Follow up: Two million people died during the Korean war, which ended with an armistice signed on the 27th July 1953. Of the 63,000 UK troops sent to Korea - many National Service conscripts - 1,078 died and more than 1,000 were taken prisoner.*
29th	Princess Elizabeth and the Duke of Edinburgh's fourteen-day-old infant daughter is named Anne Elizabeth Alice Louise. She was then known as Princess Anne of Edinburgh, and is now The Princess Royal.

SEP

7th	116 miners are trapped underground in a landslide at Knockshinnoch Castle colliery at New Cumnock in Ayrshire, Scotland. Rescue teams worked non-stop to reach the trapped men and most were eventually rescued after three days. Unfortunately 13 men trapped close to No.5 Heading however could not be reached; their bodies were recovered some months later. The disaster became an international media event.
9th	Post-war soap rationing ends.

OCT

	Alan Turing's paper 'Computing machinery and intelligence', proposing the Turing test, is published in Mind. *The Turing test is a test of a machine's ability to exhibit intelligent behaviour equivalent to, or indistinguishable from, that of a human.*
1st	In response to the British involvement in the Korean War full-time military service by conscripted National Servicemen is extended to two years.
25th	The Festival Ballet (now the English National Ballet), founded by Alicia Markova and Anton Dolin, makes its debut performance.
26th	Following its destruction by bombing in World War II, the rebuilt House of Commons is used for the first time.

NOV

15th	An attempt to hold the Second World Peace Congress at Sheffield City Hall is thwarted by the British authorities who prevent many international delegates from entering the country. It is relocated to Warsaw.

DEC

10th	Bertrand Russell wins the Nobel Prize in Literature "in recognition of his varied and significant writings in which he champions humanitarian ideals and freedom of thought".

DEC

10th — Cecil Frank Powell wins the Nobel Prize in Physics "for his development of the photographic method of studying nuclear processes and his discoveries regarding mesons made with this method".

25th December: The Stone of Scone, the traditional coronation stone of Scottish monarchs, English monarchs and more recently British monarchs, is stolen from London's Westminster Abbey by a group of four Scottish students with nationalist beliefs. It turns up in Scotland on the 11th April 1951. *Photo: The Stone of Scone being removed / recovered from Arbroath Abbey after being handed to the Custodian of the Abbey (James Wiseheart) by Scottish Nationalists.*

28th — An order to designate the Peak District as the first of the National parks of England and Wales is submitted to the Minister of Town and Country Planning for approval. The Peak District National Park, covering 555 square miles, was eventually established on the 17th April 1951.

POPULAR BRITISH PUBLICATIONS 1950

- Agatha Christie's Miss Marple novel A Murder is Announced.
- Catherine Cookson's first novel Kate Hannigan.
- William Cooper's novel Scenes from Provincial Life.
- Marion Crawford's royal biography The Little Princesses: The Story of the Queen's Childhood by her Nanny.
- Elizabeth David's recipe book A Book of Mediterranean Food.
- C. S. Forester's novel Mr. Midshipman Hornblower.
- Doris Lessing's novel The Grass is Singing.
- C. S. Lewis's novel The Lion, the Witch and the Wardrobe
- Mervyn Peake's novel Gormenghast, second of the eponymous series.
- Barbara Pym's novel Some Tame Gazelle.
- Evelyn Waugh's novel Helena.

WORLDWIDE NEWS & EVENTS

1. 1st January: The International Police Association (IPA) is founded by British police sergeant Arthur Troop (1914-2000). Today it is the largest police organisation in the world with 72 national sections and over 360,000 members.
2. 5th January: An Aeroflot twin-engined Lisunov Li-2 transport aircraft crashes in a snowstorm near Sverdlovsk airport in Russia. All 19 aboard are killed including almost the entire Soviet Air Force ice hockey team (VVS Moscow).
3. 14th January: The Soviet MiG-17 Fresco fighter aircraft makes its maiden flight. Flown by test pilot Ivan Ivashchenko (who died two months later during testing) the aircraft eventually went into service in October 1952. Including Polish and Chinese variants, a total of 10,649 of these high-subsonic aircraft were built.
4. 17th January: The Great Brinks Robbery - Thieves steal more than $2.775 million from an armoured car in Boston, Massachusetts; at the time it is the largest robbery in the history of the United States. Skilfully executed with few clues left at the crime scene, the robbery is billed as 'the crime of the century'. It was the work of an eleven-member gang, all of whom were later arrested.
5. 26th January: India promulgates its constitution and forms a republic; Rajendra Prasad is sworn in as its first president.
6. 8th February: Frank McNamara and his attorney Ralph Schneider found Diners Club International with $1.5 million. It is the world's first independent credit card company. *Fun facts: When the card was introduced Diners Club listed 27 participating restaurants and was used by just 200 of the founders' friends and acquaintances.*

7. 9th February: In a speech to the Republican Women's Club at the McClure Hotel in Wheeling, West Virginia, Senator Joseph McCarthy accuses the U.S. State Department of being filled with 205 known communists. The speech vaulted McCarthy to national prominence and sparked nationwide hysteria about subversives in the American government.

8.	9th February: The radioactive chemical element Californium (atomic number 98) is synthesized for the first time by Stanley G. Thompson, Kenneth Street, Jr., Albert Ghiorso and Glenn T. Seaborg at the University of California, Berkeley, U.S.
9.	8th March: The first Volkswagen Type 2 (Microbus) rolls off the assembly line in Wolfsburg, Germany.
10.	13th March: In Belgium a referendum over the monarchy shows 57.7% support for the return from exile of King Léopold III.

11. 23rd March: The 22nd Academy Awards ceremony is held at RKO Pantages Theatre, Hollywood, celebrating the best films from 1949. The Oscar winners include All The King's Men, Broderick Crawford and Olivia de Havilland.

12.	6th May: Tollund Man, a well-preserved naturally mummified corpse of a man who lived during the 4th century BC, is unearthed in Silkeborg, Denmark.
13.	9th May: Author of science fiction and fantasy stories L. Ron Hubbard publishes Dianetics: The Modern Science of Mental Health. *Follow up: In 1952, Hubbard lost the rights to Dianetics in bankruptcy proceedings and subsequently founded Scientology. Thereafter Hubbard oversaw the growth of the Church of Scientology into a worldwide organisation.*
14.	14th May: German-American aerospace engineer and space architect Wernher von Braun captures the public's imagination when the Huntsville Times in Alabama, U.S., runs a story with the headline, "Dr. von Braun Says Rocket Flights Possible to Moon". *Fun facts: Von Braun went on to develop the rockets that launched the United States' first space satellite, Explorer 1, and was the chief architect of the Saturn V super heavy-lift launch vehicle that propelled the Apollo spacecraft to the Moon. In 1975, in recognition of his achievements, von Braun received the U.S. National Medal of Science.*
15.	29th May: The Royal Canadian Mounted Police schooner St. Roch becomes the first ship to circumnavigate North America. *Interesting facts: In 1962 the St. Roch was designated a National Historic Site of Canada and can today be seen on display at the Vancouver Maritime Museum in British Columbia, Canada.*

16. 3rd June: Maurice Herzog and Louis Lachenal, of the French Annapurna expedition, become the first climbers to reach a summit higher than 8,000 meters; Annapurna I in Nepal (8,091m high (26,545 ft)).
17. 17th June: The first cadaveric internal kidney transplantation is performed on 44-year-old Ruth Tucker at Little Company of Mary Hospital (Evergreen Park) in Illinois, U.S. Although the donated kidney is rejected 10 months later because no effective immunosuppressive drugs have yet been developed, the intervening time gives Tucker's remaining kidney time to recover and she lives another 5 years.
18. 25th June: War breaks out in Korea when troops from the North Korean People's Army, supported by the Soviet Union and China, cross the 38th parallel into South Korea.
19. 7th July: The Group Areas Act is enacted under the apartheid government of South Africa formally segregating racial groups.
20. 16th July: 199,854 football fans watch Uruguay defeat Brazil 2-1 to win the 1950 World Cup at the Estádio do Maracanã in Rio de Janeiro. England's George Reader became the first Englishman to referee a World Cup Final and remains, to date, the oldest match official in World Cup history.

21. 24th July: A 62-feet high RTV-G-4 Bumper sounding rocket (a combination of the German V-2 rocket and the WAC Corporal sounding rocket) becomes the first ever rocket to be launched from Cape Canaveral.

22. 12th August: In his encyclical Humani generis, Pope Pius XII declares evolution to be a serious hypothesis that does not contradict essential Catholic teachings.
23. 15th August: An 8.6Mw earthquake in Assam (India) and Tibet (China) shakes the region killing approximately 4,800 people.
24. 3rd September: Italian racing driver Giuseppe Farina becomes the first winner of the FIA Formula One World Championship.

25. 18th September: Rede Tupi, the first television broadcast network in South America, is founded and launched in Brazil.

26. 2nd October: The comic strip Peanuts, written and illustrated by Charles M. Schulz, is first published in nine U.S. newspapers. *Interesting facts: At its peak in the mid to late 1960s Peanuts ran in over 2,600 newspapers and had a readership of around 355 million in 75 countries. It helped to cement the four-panel gag strip as the standard in the U.S. and, together with its merchandise, earned Schulz more than $1 billion during his lifetime. Pictured: The first ever Peanuts comic strip.*

27. 19th October: The People's Republic of China enters the Korean War after secretly sending thousands of soldiers across the Yalu River.
28. 17th November: The 14th Dalai Lama, 15-year-old Tenzin Gyatso, assumes full temporal (political) duties after the incorporation of Tibet into the People's Republic of China.
29. 24th November: Great Appalachian Storm: A phenomenal winter storm ravages the north-eastern United States bringing 30 to 50 inches of snow and temperatures below 0°F (-18°C). In all the storm impacts 22 states, kills 353 people and causes $66.7 million in damage ($669.59 million in 2019).
30. 25th November: Troops from the People's Republic of China launch a massive counterattack against South Korean and American forces long the Ch'ongch'on River Valley. These actions dash any hope for a quick end to the conflict.
31. 13th December: 19-year-old James Dean gets his first paid acting job when he makes an appearance in a Pepsi commercial.
32. 16th December: 22-year-old Shirley Temple announces her retirement from films after recent lacklustre performances.

BIRTHS
U.K. PERSONALITIES
BORN IN 1950

Peter Brian Gabriel
b. 13th February 1950

Singer, songwriter, and record producer who rose to fame as the original lead singer and flautist of the progressive rock band Genesis. After leaving Genesis in 1975, Gabriel launched a successful solo career with Solsbury Hill as his first single. His 1986 album, So, is his best-selling release and is certified triple platinum in the U.K. and five times platinum in the U.S. The album's most successful single, Sledgehammer, won a record nine MTV Awards and in 2011 was reportedly cited MTV's most played music video of all time.

Peter Gerald Hain, Baron Hain, PC
b. 16th February 1950

Labour Party politician who was the MP Neath between 1991 and 2015, and served in the Cabinets of both Tony Blair and Gordon Brown. His roles have included being the Leader of the House of Commons (2003-2005), Secretary of State for Northern Ireland (2005-2007), Secretary of State for Work and Pensions (2007-2008), and Secretary of State for Wales (2002-2008, 2009-2010). In 2014 he announced he would stand down as an MP and was nominated for a life peerage in the 2015 Dissolution Honours.

Andrew Powell
b. 19th February 1950

Guitarist, songwriter and a founding member of the rock band Wishbone Ash, a band who achieved much success in the early and mid-1970s and became known for their innovative use of twin lead guitars. Powell, alongside fellow Wishbone Ash guitarists Ted Turner and Laurie Wisefield, has been named as one of the most influential guitarists in rock music history. Today he is the sole remaining founding member of the group which has, to date, released 24 studio albums.

Dame Julia Mary Walters, DBE
b. 22nd February 1950

Actress and writer who has been the recipient of four BAFTA TV Awards, two BAFTA Film Awards, a BAFTA Fellowship and a Golden Globe. Walters came to international prominence playing the title role in the drama / comedy film Educating Rita (1983). It was a role she had created on the West End stage and it earned her an Academy Award nomination for Best Actress. On television she collaborated with Victoria Wood on several occasions and came fourth in a 2006 ITV poll of the public's 50 Greatest British TV stars.

Charles 'Roger' Pomfret Hodgson
b. 21st March 1950

Musician, singer and songwriter best known as the former co-frontman and founder member of progressive rock band Supertramp. Hodgson composed and sang the majority of the groups hits such as Dreamer, Give a Little Bit, Breakfast in America, The Logical Song and It's Raining Again. In 1984, after leaving Supertramp, he released the album In the Eye of the Storm. It became an international hit and would prove to be his biggest solo success, selling over two million copies.

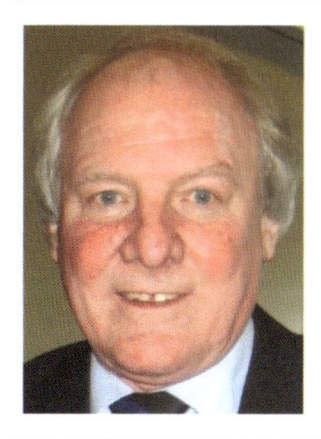

Terence Charles Yorath
b. 27th March 1950

Former footballer and manager at both club and international levels. During a playing career that lasted some 19 years he represented teams such as Leeds United, Coventry City, Tottenham Hotspur and Bradford City. Internationally he made 59 appearances for Wales (1969-1981) scoring twice. Yorath later became a football manager for Bradford City, Swansea City, Cardiff City and Sheffield Wednesday, and also managed Wales and Lebanon internationally.

Robbie Coltrane, OBE
b. 30th March 1950

Scottish actor and author born Anthony Robert McMillan. Coltrane is probably best known for his roles as Rubeus Hagrid in the Harry Potter series of films, as Valentin Dmitrovich Zukovsky in the James Bond films GoldenEye (1995) and The World Is Not Enough (1999), and as Dr. Eddie 'Fitz' Fitzgerald in the television series Cracker (for which he won BAFTAs for Best Actor in 1994, 1995 and 1996). In recognition of his services to drama he was awarded an OBE in the 2006 New Year Honours.

Sally Thomsett
b. 3rd April 1950

Actress who first came to prominence when she was cast as 11-year-old Phyllis Waterbury in the 1970 film The Railway Children (despite being 20 years old at the time). For the role she was nomination for the BAFTA Award for Most Promising Newcomer to Leading Film Roles. Other notable roles include her portrayal of Janice Hedden in the psychological thriller film Straw Dogs (1971), and playing Jo in the TV sitcom Man About the House (1973-1976).

Peter Kenneth Frampton
b. 22nd April 1950

English-American rock musician, singer, songwriter, producer and guitarist. He was previously associated with the bands Humble Pie and The Herd. As a solo artist he has released several albums including his international breakthrough album, the live release Frampton Comes Alive! The album sold more than 8 million copies in the U.S. and spawned several hit singles. He has also worked with, amongst others, Ringo Starr, David Bowie and both Matt Cameron and Mike McCready from Pearl Jam.

Daniel Fergus McGrain, MBE
b. 1st May 1950

Former professional footballer who began his career at Celtic and was one of the Quality Street Gang, a group of young players that emerged in the late 1960s. He progressed to the first team and went on to play 659 competitive games for Celtic (1970-1987), winning seven League Championships, five Scottish Cups and two Scottish League Cups. Internationally McGrain is regarded as one of Scotland's greatest players. He played in two World Cups, earnt 62 caps and was inducted to the Scottish Football Hall of Fame in 2004.

Mary Hopkin
b. 3rd May 1950

Welsh folk singer who was one of the first to sign to the Beatles' Apple label; the model Twiggy had recommended her to Paul McCartney after seeing her winning on ITV's talent show Opportunity Knocks. Her debut single, Those Were the Days, was a smash hit and sold in excess of 8 million copies globally. In March 1970 Hopkin represented the United Kingdom in the Eurovision Song Contest, finishing in second place with the song Knock, Knock, Who's There?

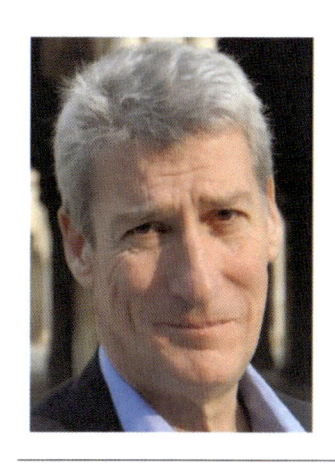

Jeremy Dickson Paxman
b. 11th May 1950

Broadcaster, journalist, author and the quizmaster of University Challenge, having succeeded Bamber Gascoigne at the time the programme was revived in 1994. Paxman joined the BBC in 1972, initially at BBC Radio Brighton, and later worked on Tonight and Panorama before becoming a newsreader for the BBC Six O'Clock News. In 1989 he began presenting BBC Two's Newsnight where he became known for his forthright and abrasive interviewing style. He left the show after 25 years in 2014.

Dame Jennifer Susan Murray, DBE
b. 12th May 1950

Journalist and broadcaster who is best known for presenting BBC Radio 4's Woman's Hour. Her career began in 1973 when she joined BBC Radio Bristol before going on to become a reporter and presenter for local news programme South Today. After a stint on BBC television's Newsnight, she then moved to Radio 4 to present the Today programme. In 1987 she took over from Sue MacGregor as the presenter of Woman's Hour, a job she continues to do as of 2019.

Alan Arthur Johnson
b. 17th May 1950

Labour Party politician who served as the MP for Hull West and Hessle from May 1997 until he stood down in May 2017. He filled a wide variety of cabinet positions in both the Blair and Brown governments including; Health Secretary, Education Secretary, Secretary of State for Work and Pensions, Secretary of State for Trade and Industry, and Home Secretary. Johnson has also published three volumes of memoirs, the first of which won the Royal Society of Literature Ondaatje Prize, and the Orwell Prize.

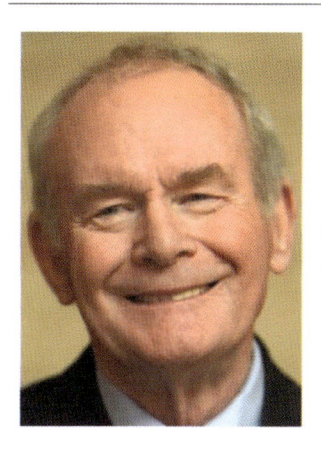

James Martin Pacelli McGuinness
b. 23rd May 1950
d. 21st March 2017

Republican Sinn Féin politician and former leader of the Provisional Irish Republican Army (IRA) terrorist group. He was an MP for Mid Ulster (1997-2013), but like all Sinn Féin MPs abstained from participation in the Westminster Parliament. Following the St Andrews Agreement in 2007 he became Northern Ireland's deputy First Minister. McGuinness was one of the main architects of the Good Friday Agreement (signed in 1998) which formally cemented the Northern Ireland peace process.

Rowan Douglas Williams, Baron Williams of Oystermouth, PC, FBA, FRSL, FLSW
b. 14th June 1950

A Welsh Anglican bishop, theologian and poet who served as the 104th Archbishop of Canterbury (2002-2012). Previously the Bishop of Monmouth and Archbishop of Wales, Williams was the first Archbishop of Canterbury in modern times not to be appointed from within the Church of England. After standing down as Archbishop, Williams took up the positions of Master of Magdalene College, Cambridge in 2013, and Chancellor of the University of South Wales in 2014.

Sir Richard Charles Nicholas Branson
b. 18th July 1950

Business magnate, investor, author and philanthropist who founded the Virgin Group. Branson's first business venture, at the age of 16, was a magazine called Student. In 1970 he set up a mail-order record business before opening a chain of Virgin Records shops. In the 1980's his Virgin brand grew rapidly, led by the expansion of his music label and the formation of the airline Virgin Atlantic. In 2004 he founded Virgin Galactic, noted for its SpaceShipTwo suborbital spaceplane designed for space tourism.

Simon John Cadell
b. 19th July 1950
d. 6th March 1996

Actor best known for his portrayal the well-meaning holiday camp manager Jeffrey Fairbrother in the BBC situation comedy Hi-de-Hi! (1980-1984), and for playing the disingenuous civil servant Dundridge in the screen adaptation of a novel by Tom Sharpe, Blott on the Landscape (1985). He also starred in the BBC sitcom Life Without George (1987-1989) and appeared on a number of other shows including; Minder, Bergerac, The Kenny Everett Television Show, and Roald Dahl's Tales of the Unexpected.

Leonard David McCluskey
b. 23rd July 1950

Trade unionist and General Secretary of Unite the Union; the largest affiliate and a major donor to the Labour Party. After leaving school he spent some years working on Liverpool Docks (for the Mersey Docks and Harbour Company) prior to becoming a full-time union official for the Transport and General Workers' Union (T&GWU) in 1979. McCluskey was elected as the General Secretary of Unite in 2010, and was re-elected to the post in 2013 and 2017.

Harriet Ruth Harman, QC
b. 30th July 1950

Solicitor and Labour Party politician who has served as an MP since 1982, first for Peckham and then for its successor constituency of Camberwell and Peckham. She has served in various Cabinet and Shadow Cabinet positions, and also served as Deputy Leader of the Labour Party and Leader of the Opposition. Harman holds the record as the longest ever continuously serving female MP in the House of Commons and as such has often been referred to as the Mother of the House.

Anne, Princess Royal, KG, KT, GCVO, QSO, CD
b. 15th August 1950

The second child and only daughter of Queen Elizabeth II and Prince Philip, Duke of Edinburgh. Anne is known for her charitable work and is a patron of over 200 organisations. She is also known for equestrian talents; she won two silver medals (1975) and one gold medal (1971) at the European Eventing Championships, and is the first member of the British Royal Family to have competed at an Olympic Games. She is currently thirteenth in the line of succession to the British throne.

Barry Steven Frank Sheene, MBE
b. 11th September 1950
d. 10th March 2003

Professional motorcycle racer who competed in Grand Prix motorcycle racing. He was a two-time world champion, winning consecutive 500cc titles in 1976 and 1977; his 1977 title remained as Britain's last solo motorcycle world championship until Danny Kent in 2015 in the Moto3 category. After a racing career stretching from 1968 to 1984, he retired from competition, relocated to Australia, and began working as a motorsport commentator and property developer.

Vicki Michelle, MBE
b. 14th December 1950

Actress and film producer best known for her role as Yvette Carte-Blanche in the BBC television comedy series 'Allo 'Allo! and as the recurring character Patricia Foster in the ITV soap opera Emmerdale. She has appeared in big-screen versions of the popular sitcoms The Likely Lads (1976) and George and Mildred (1980), and also appeared regularly in the 1970s children's television series Crackerjack. Michelle was appointed MBE in the 2010 Birthday Honours for her services to charity.

Notable Deaths

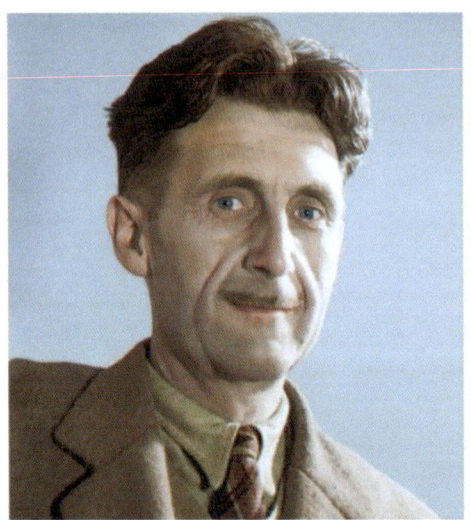

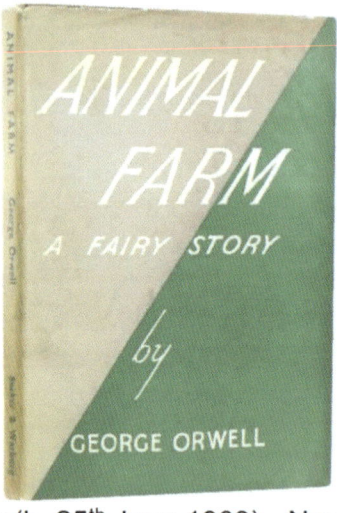

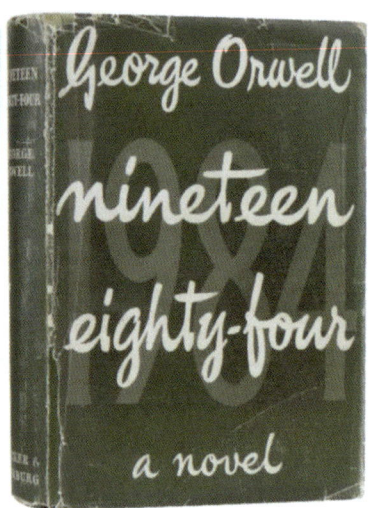

21st January 1950 - Eric Arthur Blair (b. 25th June 1903) - Novelist, essayist, journalist and critic better known by his pen name George Orwell. He wrote literary criticism, poetry, fiction and polemical journalism, and is best known for the allegorical novella Animal Farm (1945) and the dystopian novel Nineteen Eighty-Four (1949). Orwell's work continues to influence popular and political culture and the term 'Orwellian' - descriptive of totalitarian or authoritarian social practices - has entered the language together with many of his neologisms including; Big Brother, Thought Police, and Room 101. *Photos: Digitally colourised photo of George Orwell and first editions of Animal Farm / Nineteen Eighty-Four (published by Secker & Warburg, London).*

16th Feb	David Denton (b. 4th July 1874) - First-class cricketer who had a long career with Yorkshire and played eleven Tests for England. His nickname of 'Lucky' came from his habit of surviving the numerous chances that his attacking batting style naturally created for the opposition.
9th Mar	Timothy John Evans (b. 20th November 1924) - Welshman falsely convicted and hanged for the murder of his wife and infant daughter at their residence in Notting Hill, London. Three years after his execution John Christie, Evans's downstairs neighbour, was found to be a serial killer. Before his execution, Christie confessed to murdering Mrs. Evans. An official inquiry concluded in 1966 that Christie had also murdered Evans's daughter, and Evans was granted a posthumous pardon. The case generated much controversy and is acknowledged as a serious miscarriage of justice. Along with those of Derek Bentley and Ruth Ellis, the case played a major part in the abolition of capital punishment for murder in the United Kingdom in 1965.
19th Mar	Sir Walter Norman Haworth, FRS (b. 19th March 1883) - Chemist best known for his ground-breaking work on ascorbic acid (vitamin C) while working at the University of Birmingham. He received the 1937 Nobel Prize in Chemistry "for his investigations on carbohydrates and vitamin C".
24th Mar	Harold Joseph Laski (b. 30th June 1893) - Political theorist, economist, author, and lecturer. He was active in politics and served as the chairman of the British Labour Party during 1945 and 1946, and was a professor at the London School of Economics from 1926 to 1950.

30th Mar	Ninnian Joseph Yule (b. 30th April 1892) - Scottish-American burlesque and vaudeville comedian who later appeared in many films as a character actor. He was noted for his starring role in the Jiggs and Maggie film series, opposite Renie Riano, and as the father of Mickey Rooney.
19th Apr	Gerald Hugh Tyrwhitt-Wilson, 14th Baron Berners (b. 18th September 1883) - Composer, novelist, painter and aesthete also known as Gerald Tyrwhitt.
24th May	Field Marshal Archibald Percival Wavell, 1st Earl Wavell, GCB, GCSI, GCIE, CMG, MC, KStJ, PC (b. 5th May 1883) - Senior officer in the British Army who served in the Second Boer War, the Bazar Valley Campaign and World War I. During the Second World War he served as Commander-in-Chief Middle East and Commander-in-Chief, India. From September 1943, until his retirement in February 1947, he was the Governor-General and Viceroy of India.
28th Jun	Henry Balfour Gardiner (b. 7th November 1877) - Musician, composer and teacher who is best known for his anthem Evening Hymn, 'Te lucis ante terminum'.
17th Jul	General Evangeline Cory Booth, OF (b. 25th December 1865) - Theologian and the 4th General of The Salvation Army (1934-1939). She was the first woman to hold the post of General.
29th Jul	Joseph Gibson Fry (b. 26th October 1915) - Racing driver and distant member of the Fry's Chocolate family. He became the primary driver for the highly successful Shelsley Special 'Freikaiserwagen', created by his cousin David Fry and Hugh Dunsterville.
6th Sep	William Olaf Stapledon (b. 10th May 1886) - Philosopher and author of science fiction who was inducted into the Science Fiction and Fantasy Hall of Fame in 2014.
21st Sep	Edward Arthur Milne, FRS (b. 14th February 1896) - Astrophysicist, mathematician and author who was President of the Royal Astronomical Society (1943-1945).
2nd Nov	George Bernard Shaw (b. 26th July 1856) - Playwright, critic, polemicist and political activist. His influence on Western theatre, culture and politics extended from the 1880s to his death and beyond. He wrote more than sixty plays, including major works such as Man and Superman (1902), Pygmalion (1912) and Saint Joan (1923). With a range incorporating both contemporary satire and historical allegory, Shaw became the leading dramatist of his generation and in 1925 was awarded the Nobel Prize in Literature.
12th Nov	Julia Marlowe (b. Sarah Frances Frost; 17th August 1865) - English-born American actress and suffragist known for her interpretations of William Shakespeare.
23rd Nov	Thomas Percival Montague Mackey (b. 1st June 1894) - Pianist, composer and bandleader better known as Percival Mackey. He is particularly known for his work as a composer and musical director for films during the 1930s and 1940s.
28th Nov	James Henry 'Tish' Corbitt (b. 1913) - Murderer hanged at Strangeways Prison in Manchester by Albert Pierrepoint. Corbitt knew his hangman before carrying out the murder of his mistress, Eliza Woods, and was a frequent customer in Pierrepoint's pub, Help The Poor Struggler. Corbitt had sang with him round the piano at the pub, and called him 'Tosh' while Pierrepoint called him 'Tish'.
25th Dec	Neil L. M. Francis Hawkins (b. 1903) - Leading British fascist, both before and after the Second World War. He played a leading role in the British Union of Fascists, controlling the organisational structure of the movement.

POPULAR MUSIC

Nat King Cole	No.1	Mona Lisa
Anton Karas	No.2	The Third Man Theme
Teresa Brewer	No.3	Music, Music, Music
Gordon Jenkins & The Weavers	No.4	Goodnight, Irene
Doris Day	No.5	Bewitched
Billy Eckstine	No.6	My Foolish Heart
Dinah Shore	No.7	Dear Hearts & Gentle People
Bing Crosby	No.8	Rudolph, The Red-Nosed Reindeer
The Ink Spots	No.9	You're Breaking My Heart
Eve Young & The Homesteaders	No.10	Silver Dollar

N.B. The first British record sales chart, The Hit Parade, did not appear until 14th November 1952. Prior to this popular songs were measured by sales of sheet music which was purchased both by professional musicians who performed live in pubs, clubs and theatres, and by keen amateurs. A song could often be perfomed by many different combinations of singers and bands, and the contemporary charts would list the song without clarifying whose version was the major hit. With this in mind it should be noted that although the above chart has been compiled with best intent it remains subjective.

Nat King Cole
Mona Lisa

Label:	Written by:	Length:
Capitol Records	Jay Livingston / Ray Evans	3 mins 12 secs

Nathaniel Adams Coles (b. 17th March 1919 - d. 15th February 1965) was a singer, actor and television host known professionally as Nat King Cole. He first came to prominence as a leading jazz pianist, and then gained further popularity with his soft baritone voice performing in the big band and jazz genres. By the 1950s Cole emerged as a solo performer and scored numerous hits with such songs as; Nature Boy, Mona Lisa, Too Young, and Unforgettable.

Anton Karas
The Third Man Theme

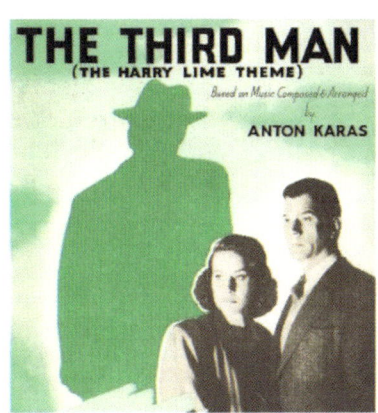

Label:	Written by:	Length:
Decca	Anton Karas	2 mins 6 secs

Anton Karas (b. 7th July 1906 - d. 10th January 1985) was a Viennese zither player and composer, best known for his internationally famous soundtrack to Carol Reed's The Third Man (1949). The film, with the music a contributing factor, was a gigantic success, and Karas' life was changed drastically. As a result, he toured all over the world and performed for many celebrities including the British royal family.

3 Teresa Brewer
Music, Music, Music

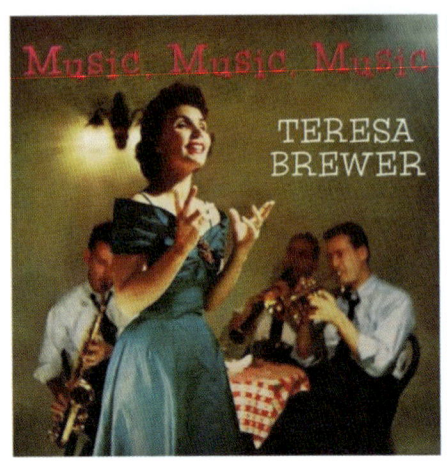

Label:	Written by:	Length:
London Records	Weiss / Baum	2 mins 20 secs

Teresa Brewer (b. Theresa Veronica Breuer; 7th May 1931 - d. 17th October 2007) was an American singer whose style incorporated country, jazz, R&B, musicals, and novelty songs. She was one of the most prolific and popular female singers of the 1950s, recording nearly 600 songs. Her No.1 hit Music, Music, Music went on to sell over a million copies and earned her the nickname Miss Music.

---

4 Gordon Jenkins & The Weavers
Goodnight, Irene

Label:	Written by:	Length:
Decca	Ledbetter / Lomax	3 mins 19 secs

Gordon Hill Jenkins (b. 12th May 1910 - d. 1st May 1984) was an arranger, composer and pianist who was an influential figure in popular music in the 1940s and 1950s. Jenkins discovered and was instrumental in **The Weavers** (Ronnie Gilbert, Lee Hays, Fred Hellerman, and Pete Seeger) getting a recording contract. Shortly after signing with Decca they made it to No.1 with their version of Lead Belly's 1943 hit Goodnight, Irene.

5. Doris Day
Bewitched

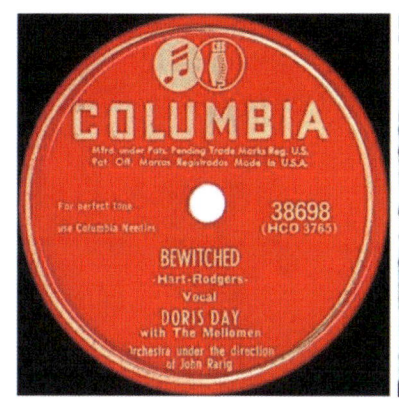

Label:	Written by:	Length:
Columbia	Hart / Rodgers	2 mins 44 secs

Doris Day (b. 3rd April 1922 - d. 13th May 2019) is an actress, singer and animal rights activist. Day began her career as a big band singer in 1939. Her popularity began to rise after her first hit recording, Sentimental Journey, in 1945. After, when Day embarked on a solo career, she started her long-lasting partnership with Columbia Records (1947-1967). Distributed by Philips in the UK, Day made more than 650 recordings and became one of the most popular singers of the 20th century.

6. Billy Eckstine
My Foolish Heart

Label:	Written by:	Length:
MGM Records	Young / Washington	3 mins 3 secs

William Clarence Eckstine (b. 8th July 1914 - d. 8th March 1993) was a jazz and pop singer, and a bandleader of the swing era. He was noted for his rich, resonant, almost operatic bass-baritone voice. My Foolish Heart was introduced by the singer Martha Mears in the 1949 film of the same name. The song was subsequently released by a number of recording artists at the time, but it was Eckstein's version which proved most popular selling in excess of one million copies.

7. Dinah Shore
Dear Hearts & Gentle People

Label: Columbia | **Written by:** Saxon / Wells | **Length:** 2 mins 43 secs

Dinah Shore (b. Frances Rose Shore; 29th February 1916 - d. 24th February 1994) was a singer, actress, television personality and the top-charting female vocalist during the Big Band era of the 1940s and 1950s. After failing singing auditions for the bands of Benny Goodman, Jimmy Dorsey and his brother Tommy Dorsey, Shore struck out on her own and became the first singer of her era to achieve huge solo success.

8. Bing Crosby
Rudolph, The Red-Nosed Reindeer

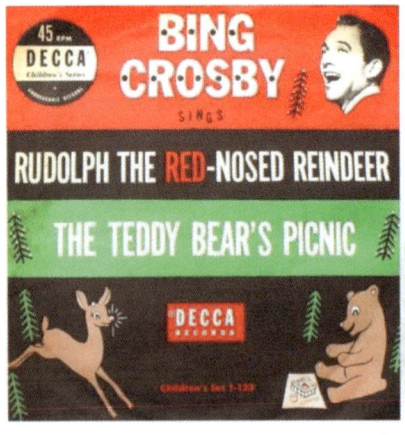

Label: Brunswick / Decca | **Written by:** Johnny Marks | **Length:** 2 mins 15 secs

Harry Lillis 'Bing' Crosby, Jr. (b. 3rd May 1903 - d. 14th October 1977) was a singer and actor who was a leader in record sales, radio ratings, and motion picture grosses from 1931 to 1954. Crosby's trademark warm bass-baritone voice made him the best-selling recording artist of the 20th century, selling close to a billion records, tapes, compact discs, and digital downloads worldwide.

The Ink Spots
You're Breaking My Heart

Label:	Written by:	Length:
Brunswick / Decca	Genaro / Skylar	3 mins 21 sec

The Ink Spots, whose most prominent members were Bill Kenny (b. 12th June 1914 - d. 23rd March 1978), Deek Watson (b. 18th July 1909 - d. 4th November 1969), Charlie Fuqua (b. 20th October 1910 - d. 21st December 1971), and Hoppy Jones (b. 17th February 1905 - d. 18th October 1944), were a pop vocal group who gained international fame in the 1930s and 1940s. In 1989 the Ink Spots were inducted into the Rock and Roll Hall of Fame, and in 1999 they were inducted into the Vocal Group Hall of Fame.

Eve Young & The Homesteaders
Silver Dollar

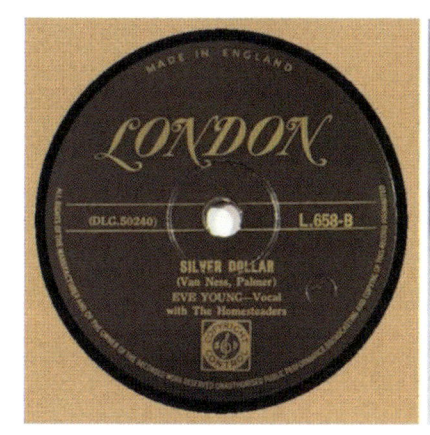

Label:	Written by:	Length:
London Records	Van Ness / Palmer	2 mins 44 secs

Eve Young (b. Eva Nadauld; 1st September 1923 - d. 3rd November 2010), also known later in her career as Karen Chandler, was an American singer of popular music during the 1940s, 1950s and 1960s. Her biggest successes came in 1950 with Silver Dollar and (If I Knew You Were Comin') I'd've Baked A Cake, both of which reached the top of the British sheet music charts.

1950: TOP FILMS

1. **King Solomon's Mines** - *MGM*
2. **All About Eve** - *20th Century Fox*
3. **Cinderella** - *Disney*
4. **Annie Get Your Gun** - *MGM*
5. **Father Of The Bride** - *MGM*

OSCARS

Best Picture: All About Eve
Most Nominations: All About Eve (14)
Most Wins: All About Eve (6)

Photo 1: Presenter Gloria Swanson (left) with Best Actor / Actress winners José Ferrer and Judy Holliday. Photo 2: Joseph L. Mankiewicz - Best Director.

Best Director: Joseph L. Mankiewicz - *All About Eve*

Best Actor: José Ferrer - *Cyrano de Bergerac*
Best Actress: Judy Holliday - *Born Yesterday*
Best Supporting Actor: George Sanders - *All About Eve*
Best Supporting Actress: Josephine Hull - *Harvey*

The 23rd Academy Awards were presented on the 29th March 1951.

King Solomon's Mines

Directed by: Compton Bennett / Andrew Marton - Runtime: 1 hour 43 minutes

Adventurer Allan Quartermain leads an expedition into uncharted African territory in an attempt to locate an explorer who went missing during his search for the fabled diamond mines of King Solomon.

STARRING

Deborah Kerr, CBE
b. 30th September 1921
d. 16th October 2007

Character:
Elizabeth Curtis

Scottish film, theatre and television actress. Kerr won a Golden Globe for her performance as Anna Leonowens in The King and I, and the Sarah Siddons Award for her performance as Laura Reynolds in the play Tea and Sympathy. She was also a three-time winner of the New York Film Critics Circle Award for Best Actress and was nominated six times for the Academy Award for Best Actress but never won.

Stewart Granger
b. 6th May 1913
d. 16th August 1993

Character:
Allan Quatermain

Stewart Granger was an English film actor mainly associated with heroic and romantic leading roles. Born James Lablache Stewart, he made his film debut as an extra in The Song You Gave Me (1933). Granger was a popular leading man from the 1940s to the early 1960s, rising to fame through his appearances in the Gainsborough melodramas.

Richard Carlson
b. 29th April 1912
d. 25th November 1977

Character:
John Goode

American actor, television and film director, and screenwriter who made his acting debut on Broadway in Three Men On A Horse (1935). His first film role was in the 1938 David O. Selznick comedy The Young In Heart. From then until 1969 he went on to star in a further 55 films, mainly as a supporting actor. Carlson is perhaps best remembered for his role in the TV series I Led 3 Lives (1953-1956).

TRIVIA

Goofs | Von Brun (when Allan, Elizabeth and John first meet him) states that he hasn't seen a white face in five years, but immediately after tells them that he saw Curtis a year earlier. Neither of the three question this inconsistency.

During the stampede, when zebras run past the hiding safari members, two trucks being used to herd the animals can clearly be seen through the dust in the rear of the shot.

Interesting Facts | The Deborah Kerr character, Elizabeth Curtis, is a screenwriter's invention and does not appear in H. Rider Haggard's original novel.

CONTINUED

Interesting Facts — Errol Flynn was originally cast as Quartermain but turned it down as he did not want to sleep in a tent on location in Africa. Instead he did Kim (1950), which was filmed in India but the accommodation for the actors was at a local resort.

The scene in which Deborah Kerr cuts her own hair, and then cuts to her sunning herself with a perfectly coiffed hairstyle, got such a big laugh at the initial screenings of the film that producers debated removing the scene. However, they couldn't figure out another way to explain Kerr's change of hairstyle so they kept the improbable scenes intact.

The location footage in this film, especially the various animals, was re-used as stock footage for dozens of motion pictures in the fifties and later. This includes films such as; Tarzan, The Ape Man (1959), Watusi (1959), and the 1973 version of Trader Horn.

While filming on location in Carlsbad National Park's New Cave, Deborah Kerr took her lipstick and wrote the initials DK on a cave formation near the Klansman formation that was used as a background. An electrician also took a burned-out lamp and tossed it in a hole under that formation. Since the cave is still 'active', meaning the formations are still slowly being encased in more minerals, the initials and the lamp are now solidly encased in a layer limestone that is thin enough to see through but thick enough to prevent removal. The Carlsbad Park Rangers refer to the DK as the Deborah Kerr formation. Both are still visible to this day.

Quote — **Allan Quatermain:** ...in the end you begin to accept it all... you watch things hunting and being hunted, reproducing, killing and dying, it's all endless and pointless, except in the end one small pattern emerges from it all, the only certainty: one is born, one lives for a time then one dies, that is all...

All About Eve

Directed by: Joseph L. Mankiewicz - Runtime: 2 hours 18 minutes

An ingenue insinuates herself into the lives of an established but aging stage actress and her circle of theatre friends.

STARRING

Ruth Elizabeth 'Bette' Davis
b. 5th April 1908
d. 6th October 1989

Character:
Margo Channing

Actress of film, television, and theatre. With a career spanning 60 years, she is regarded as one of the greatest actresses in Hollywood history. She won the Academy Award for Best Actress twice, was the first person to accrue 10 Academy Award nominations for acting, and was the first woman to receive a Lifetime Achievement Award from the American Film Institute.

Anne Baxter
b. 7th May 1923
d. 12th December 1985

Character:
Eve Harrington

Actress of stage and screen. Baxter won the Academy Award for Best Supporting Actress for her role as Sophie in the 1946 film The Razor's Edge, and also received an Academy Award nomination for Best Actress for the title role in All About Eve. Other notable film performances include; The Magnificent Ambersons (1942), I Confess (1953), and The Ten Commandments (1956).

George Sanders
b. 3rd July 1906
d. 25th April 1972

Character:
Addison DeWitt

British film and television actor, singer-songwriter, music composer, and author. His career as an actor spanned over forty years and included roles in films such as; Rebecca (1940), Foreign Correspondent (1940), All About Eve, for which he won the Academy Award for Best Supporting Actor, and Ivanhoe (1952). Sanders has two stars on the Hollywood Walk of Fame, for films and television.

TRIVIA

Goofs | When Karen, Bill and Margo are returning from a long weekend in the country and they run out of petrol, the fuel gauge still shows that the tank is just under half full.

While Phoebe is looking at herself in the mirror during the final scene, a crew member sitting on a crane is visible for a few seconds at the top of the shot.

Interesting Facts | All About Eve shares the record for the most Oscar nominations (14) with Titanic (1997) and La La Land (2016).

CONTINUED

Interesting Facts

This was the first time two actresses from one film were both Oscar nominated for Best Actress. Anne Baxter had lobbied heavily to be nominated in the best actress category rather than as a supporting actress. By doing so she may have cost both herself and Bette Davis the award.

During the making of the film Zsa Zsa Gabor kept arriving on the set because she was jealous of her husband George Sanders in his scenes with the young blonde ingenue Marilyn Monroe.

Bette Davis fell in love with her co-star Gary Merrill during the shooting of this movie and the two married in July 1950, a few weeks after filming was completed. They adopted a baby girl whom they named Margot.

Co-star Celeste Holm spoke about her experience with Bette Davis on the first day of shooting: "I walked onto the set... on the first day and said, 'Good morning,' and do you know her reply? She said, 'Oh shit, good manners.' I never spoke to her again - ever."

Years after making the picture Bette Davis said in an interview "Filming All About Eve (1950) was a very happy experience... the only bitch in the cast was Celeste Holm".

Quotes

Birdie: There's a message from the bartender. Does Miss Channing know she ordered domestic gin by mistake?
Margo: The only thing I ordered by mistake is the guests. They're domestic too, and they don't care what they drink as long as it burns!

Margo: Fasten your seatbelts, it's going to be a bumpy night!

CINDERELLA

For All the World to LOVE!

WALT DISNEY'S CINDERELLA

A LOVE STORY WITH MUSIC

Greatest since SNOW WHITE

Color by TECHNICOLOR

Distributed by RKO Radio Pictures, Inc.

Directors: Geronimi / Jackson / Luske - Runtime: 1 hour 14 minutes

When Cinderella's cruel stepmother prevents her from attending the Royal Ball, she gets some unexpected help from the lovable mice Gus and Jaq, and from her Fairy Godmother.

STARRING

Jacqueline Ruth 'Ilene' Woods
b. 5th May 1929
d. 1st July 2010

Character:
Cinderella (voice)

Actress and singer who is primarily known as the original voice of the title character of the Walt Disney animated feature Cinderella, for which she was named a Disney Legend in 2003. The role came about when two of her songwriter friends, Mack David and Jerry Livingston, called her to record 3 songs from the film. They then presented them to Walt Disney and two days later he asked her to voice the role of Cinderella.

Eleanor Audley
b. 19th November 1905
d. 25th November 1991

Character:
Lady Tremaine (voice)

Actress who had a distinctive voice in radio and animation, in addition to her TV and film roles. She is best remembered on television as Oliver Douglas's mother, Eunice Douglas, on the CBS sitcom, Green Acres (1965-1969), and for providing Disney animated features with the villainess voices of Lady Tremaine in Cinderella (1950), and Maleficent in Sleeping Beauty (1959).

Verna Felton
b. 20th July 1890
d. 14th December 1966

Character:
Fairy Godmother (voice)

Actress who was best known for providing many voices in numerous Disney animated films, as well as voicing Fred Flintstone's mother-in-law Pearl Slaghoople in Hanna-Barbera's The Flintstones (1962-1963). Two of her other most famous roles were as Mrs. Day on The Jack Benny Program (1939-1962) and as Hilda Crocker on the CBS sitcom December Bride (1952-1959).

TRIVIA

Goofs | Whilst Cinderella is singing So This Is Love, she dips her hand the fountain wearing full-length evening gloves.

When Cinderella and the Prince are dancing, just before they go out into the garden, they cast large shadows onto the wall. These shadows do not match their movements.

Interesting Facts | The transformation of Cinderella's torn dress to that of the white ball gown was considered to be Walt Disney's favourite piece of animation.

CONTINUED

Interesting Facts

Lucifer was modelled after animator Ward Kimball's cat, a plump, six-toed calico named Feetsy. To prepare for Cinderella Kimball had studied dozens of cats but was having trouble coming up with an effective design for the villainous feline. One day Walt Disney visited the animator's home to talk shop, and Feetsy persisted in brushing against Walt's legs throughout the conversation. Walt, who was not fond of cats, finally declared, "For gosh sakes, Kimball, there's your Lucifer right here!"

Cinderella loses a shoe three times in the film: first, when she delivers the breakfast trays (causing Lucifer to look under the wrong cup), second, when she is running away from the ball, and lastly, on her wedding day running down the steps.

Ilene Woods suffered from Alzheimer's disease in the later years of her life. During this time, she did not even remember that she had played Cinderella, but nurses claimed that she was very much comforted by her song from the film, A Dream Is A Wish Your Heart Makes.

Quote

[as Cinderella prepares to try on the slipper]
Grand Duke: Come, my child.
[beckons to the Page Boy, who runs carrying the slipper. The stepmother sticks out her cane and trips him, causing the slipper to shatter into pieces]
Grand Duke: Oh, no! Oh, no, no. Oh, no. Oh, this is terrible. The King! What will he say? What will he *do*?
Cinderella: But, perhaps, if it would help...
Grand Duke: *[sobbing]* No, no, nothing can help now. Nothing!
Cinderella: [bringing out the other glass slipper] But, you see, I have the other slipper.

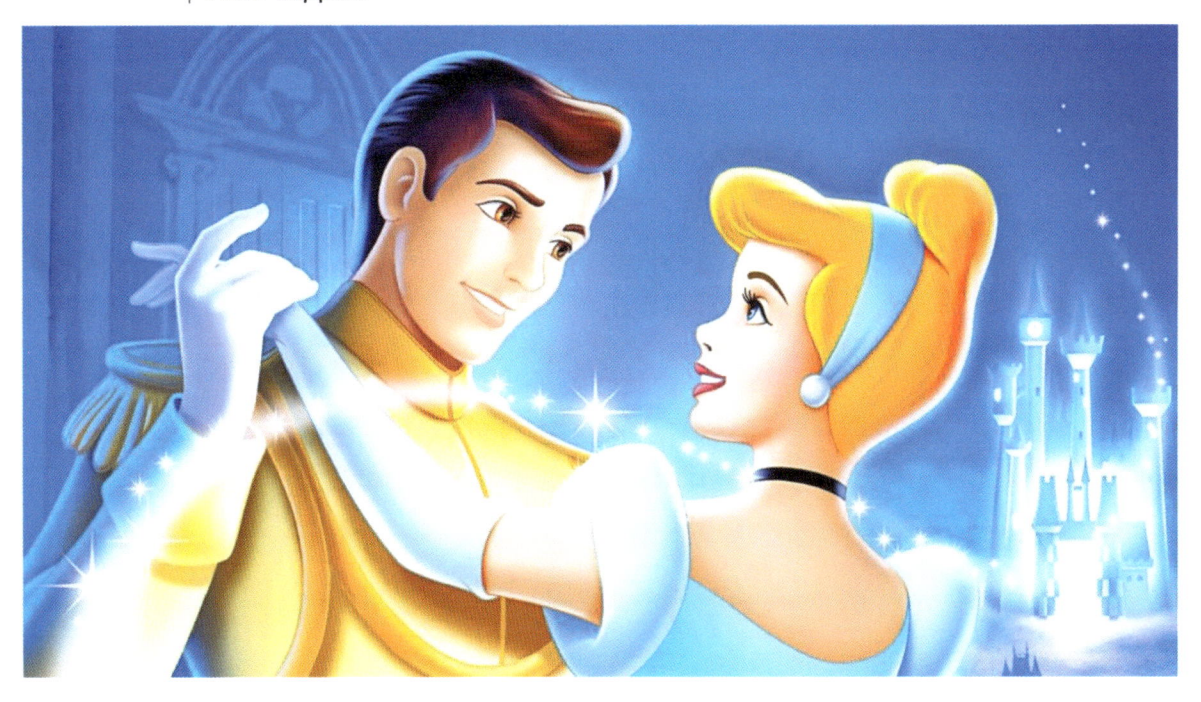

ANNIE GET YOUR GUN

Directed by: Charles Chaplin - Runtime: 2 hours 5 minutes

A film loosely based on the story of sharpshooter Annie Oakley and her love and professional rivalry with Frank Butler.

STARRING

Betty Hutton
b. 26th February 1921
d. 12th March 2007

Character:
Annie Oakley

Stage, film and television actress, comedian, dancer and singer born Elizabeth June Thornburg. Her film career began when she was signed by Paramount Pictures and appeared in the films The Fleet's In (1942), and The Miracle of Morgan's Creek (1944). Her biggest success though came when playing Annie Oakley in the MGM musical Annie Get Your Gun.

Harry Clifford Keel
b. 13th April 1919
d. 7th November 2004

Character:
Frank Butler

Actor and singer, known professionally as Howard Keel, who starred in a number of MGM musicals in the 1950s, and in the CBS television series Dallas (1981-1991). Success in Dallas renewed his singing career and in 1984, aged 64, he reached No.6 in the UK Albums Chart with the record 'And I Love You So'. For his contribution to motion pictures Keel received a star on the Hollywood Walk of Fame in 1960.

Louis Calhern
b. 19th February 1895
d. 12th May 1956

Character:
Buffalo Bill Cody

Stage and screen actor born Carl Henry Vogt. He began working in silent films for director Lois Weber in the early 1920s; the most notable being The Blot (1921). In 1923, Calhern left the movies to devote his career entirely to the stage, but returned after eight years with the advent of sound pictures. He was nominated for an Oscar for Best Actor for his role in the film The Magnificent Yankee (1950).

TRIVIA

Goofs | Annie sees the Statue of Liberty as she returns to America to win Frank Butler's heart. The statue wasn't completed in New York harbour until 1886, four years after Frank and Annie's actual wedding.

During the shooting match between Annie and Frank, a number of the clay targets actually explode before the shot has been taken, and several are hit despite the rifle not even pointed at the target (most noticeably on Annie's first shot). In addition, neither shooter stops to reload their rifles despite a continuous barrage of firing.

CONTINUED

Interesting Facts

Ginger Rogers wrote in her 1991 autobiography that she told her agent Leland Hayward to aggressively go after this film for her, and that money was no object. She wrote that she would have worked for one dollar to make it legal. Hayward spoke with Louis B. Mayer, who said: "Tell Ginger to stay in her high-heel shoes and her silk stockings, she could never be as rambunctious as Annie Oakley has to be".

Betty Hutton and Howard Keel did not get along during filming. Keel thought that Hutton cared more about her career than her co-stars.

Judy Garland and Frank Morgan, who appeared together in The Wizard of Oz (1939), were scheduled to reappear together in this film. Garland was fired because of health problems, and Frank Morgan died shortly after filming began. As a result of this, Betty Hutton took over Judy Garland's role as Annie Oakley, and Louis Calhern succeeded Frank Morgan as William F. Cody aka Buffalo Bill.

FATHER OF THE BRIDE

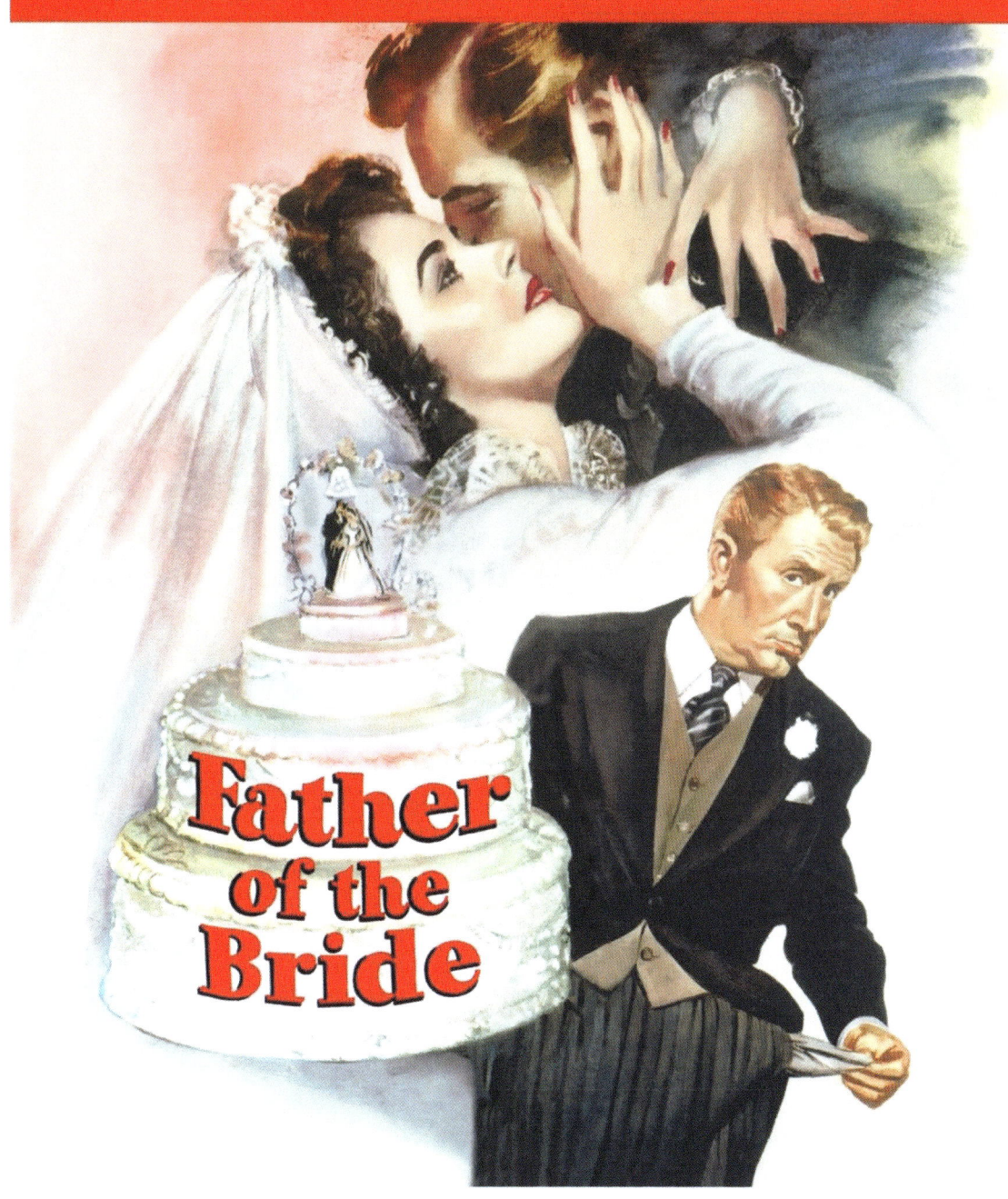

SPENCER TRACY   **JOAN BENNETT**   **ELIZABETH TAYLOR**

Directed by: Vincente Minnelli - Runtime: 1 hour 32 minutes

The father of a young woman deals with the emotional pain of her getting married, along with the financial and organisational trouble of arranging the wedding.

STARRING

Spencer Tracy
b. 1st April 1900
d. 10th June 1967

Character:
Stanley T. Banks

Spencer Bonaventure Tracy was an actor noted for his natural style and versatility. One of the major stars of Hollywood's Golden Age, he appeared in 75 films and developed a reputation among his peers as one of the screen's greatest actors. Tracy was nominated for nine Academy Awards for Best Actor, winning two and sharing the record for total nominations with Laurence Olivier.

Joan Geraldine Bennett
b. 27th February 1910
d. 7th December 1990

Characters:
Ellie Banks

Stage, film and television actress who appeared in more than 70 films over a period of 60 years. She is possibly best-remembered for her film noir femme fatale roles in director Fritz Lang's movies such as; Man Hunt (1941), The Woman In The Window (1944) and Scarlet Street (1945). In the 1960s, she achieved further success for her portrayal of Elizabeth Collins Stoddard on TV's Dark Shadows.

Elizabeth Taylor
b. 27th February 1932
d. 23rd March 2011

Character:
Kay Banks

Dame Elizabeth Taylor was a British-American actress who from her early years as a child star with MGM became one of the greatest screen actresses of Hollywood's Golden Age. In total Taylor was nominated for 5 Academy Awards for Best Actress, winning on two occasions for her roles in BUtterfield 8 (1960) and Who's Afraid of Virginia Woolf? (1966).

TRIVIA

Goofs | When the Bank's are driving to meet Buckley's parents, Ellie says they are looking for the house numbered 394. When they get to the destination, the number on the house is 709.

At the party to announce the engagement, Stanley is fixing drinks, and opens two Cokes which spray all over him. In both cases it is obvious that the spray is coming from the wall cabinet, not from the coke bottle.

Interesting Facts | Father Of The Bride was the only Best Picture Oscar nominee for 1950 not to win any Academy Awards.

CONTINUED

Interesting Facts Spencer Tracy wanted Katharine Hepburn for his screen wife, but it was felt that they were too romantic a team to play a happily domesticated couple with children, so Joan Bennett got the part.

The premiere of this film took place six weeks after Elizabeth Taylor's real-life marriage to 'Nicky' Conrad Hilton Jr. The publicity surrounding the event is credited with helping to make the film so successful.

MGM gave 18-year-old Elizabeth Taylor a wedding gift of a one-off wedding dress designed by legendary costumier Helen Rose (a move also designed to promote the film).

Quote **Stanley T. Banks:** You fathers will understand. You have a little girl. She looks up to you. You're her oracle. You're her hero. And then the day comes when she gets her first permanent wave and goes to her first real party, and from that day on you're in a constant state of panic.

Sporting Winners

Five Nations Rugby
Wales

Position	Nation	Played	Won	Draw	Lost	For	Against	+/-	Points
1	**Wales**	4	4	0	0	50	8	+42	8
2	Scotland	4	2	0	2	21	49	-28	4
3	Ireland	4	1	1	2	27	12	+15	3
4	France	4	1	1	2	14	35	-21	3
5	England	4	1	0	3	22	30	-8	2

The 1950 Five Nations Championship was the twenty-first series of the rugby union Five Nations Championship. Including the previous incarnations as the Home Nations and Five Nations, this was the fifty-sixth series of the northern hemisphere rugby union championship. Ten matches were played between the 14th January and 25th March, with Wales winning its 11th title, the Grand Slam and Triple Crown.

Date	Team	Score	Team	Location
14-01-1950	Scotland	8-5	France	Edinburgh
21-01-1950	England	5-11	Wales	London
28-01-1950	France	3-3	Ireland	Colombes
04-02-1950	Wales	12-0	Scotland	Cardiff
11-02-1950	England	3-0	Ireland	London
25-02-1950	France	6-3	England	Colombes
25-02-1950	Ireland	21-0	Scotland	Dublin
11-03-1950	Ireland	3-6	Wales	Belfast
18-03-1950	Scotland	13-11	England	Edinburgh
25-03-1950	Wales	21-0	France	Cardiff

Calcutta Cup

Scotland 13-11 England

The Calcutta Cup was first awarded in 1879 and is the rugby union trophy awarded to the winner of the match (currently played as part of the Six Nations Championship) between England and Scotland. The Cup was presented to the Rugby Football Union after the Calcutta Football Club in India disbanded in 1878; it is made from melted down silver rupees withdrawn from the club's funds.

British Grand Prix - Giuseppe Farina

Giuseppe Farina competing in the 1950 British Grand Prix at Silverstone.

The 1950 British Grand Prix was held at Silverstone on the 13th May. The race was won by 43-year-old Giuseppe Farina, from pole position, over 70 laps of the 2.89-mile circuit. Farina also claimed the fastest lap with a time of 1m 50.6s.

Pos.	Country	Driver	Car
1	**Italy**	**Giuseppe Farina**	**Alfa Romeo**
2	Italy	Luigi Fagioli	Alfa Romeo
3	United Kingdom	Reg Parnell	Alfa Romeo

Silverstone first hosted the British Grand Prix in 1948 and is built on the site of the World War II Royal Air Force bomber station, RAF Silverstone. The airfield's three runways, in a classic WWII triangular format, lie within the outline of the present track.

1950 Grand Prix Season

Date	Race	Circuit	Winning Driver	Constructor
13-05	British Grand Prix	Silverstone	Giuseppe Farina	Alfa Romeo
21-05	Monaco Grand Prix	Monaco	Juan Manuel Fangio	Alfa Romeo
30-05	Indianapolis 500	Indianapolis	Johnnie Parsons	Kurtis Kraft
04-06	Swiss Grand Prix	Bremgarten	Giuseppe Farina	Alfa Romeo
18-06	Belgian Grand Prix	Spa	Juan Manuel Fangio	Alfa Romeo
02-07	French Grand Prix	Reims-Gueux	Juan Manuel Fangio	Alfa Romeo
03-09	Italian Grand Prix	Monza	Giuseppe Farina	Alfa Romeo

The 1950 Formula One season was the fourth season of the FIA's Formula One motor racing. It featured the inaugural FIA World Championship of Drivers as well as a number of non-championship races. Giuseppe Farina won the championship with 30 points from Juan Manuel Fangio (27) and Luigi Fagioli (24); all three drove for Alfa Romeo.

Grand National - Freebooter

The 1950 Grand National was the 104th renewal of this world famous horse race and took place at Aintree Racecourse near Liverpool on the 25th March. The winning horse was Freebooter, who was trained by Bobby Renton and ridden by jockey Jimmy Power. Forty-nine horses contested the race in front of the King and Queen and nearly 500,000 race fans. Of the 49 runners only 7 horses completed the course; 33 fell, 4 pulled up, 2 were brought down, 2 refused and 1 unseated the rider. All the horses returned safely to the stables afterwards.

	Horse	Jockey	Age	Weight	Odds
1st	**Freebooter**	**Jimmy Power**	9	**11st-11lb**	**10/1**
2nd	Wot No Sun	Arthur Thompson	8	11st-8lb	100/7
3rd	Acthon Major	Bobby O'Ryan	10	11st-2lb	33/1
4th	Rowland Roy	Dicky Black	11	11st-7lb	40/1
5th	Monaveen	Tony Grantham	9	10st-13lb	100/7

Epsom Derby - Galcador

The Derby Stakes is Britain's richest horse race and the most prestigious of the country's five Classics. First run in 1780 this Group 1 flat horse race is open to 3-year-old thoroughbred colts and fillies. The race takes place at Epsom Downs in Surrey over a distance of one mile, four furlongs and 10 yards (2,423 metres) and is scheduled for early June each year.

Photo: French Thoroughbred racehorse Galcador (1947-1970) seen being led in after winning the 1950 Epsom Derby. The horse was owned by Marcel Boussac and ridden by Rae Johnstone.

Football League Champions

England

Pos.	Team	W	D	L	F	A	Pts.
1	**Portsmouth**	**22**	**9**	**11**	**74**	**38**	**53**
2	Wolverhampton Wanderers	20	13	9	76	49	53
3	Sunderland	21	10	11	83	62	52
4	Manchester United	18	14	10	69	44	50
5	Newcastle United	19	12	11	77	55	50

Scotland

Pos.	Team	W	D	L	F	A	Pts.
1	**Rangers**	**22**	**6**	**2**	**58**	**26**	**50**
2	Hibernian	22	5	3	86	34	49
3	Hearts	20	3	7	86	40	43
4	East Fife	15	7	8	58	43	37
5	Celtic	14	7	9	51	50	35

FA Cup Winners - Arsenal

Arsenal 2-0 Liverpool

The 1950 FA Cup Final took place on the 29th April at Wembley Stadium in front of 100,000 fans. Arsenal won the match to take the Cup for the third time; both goals were scored by Reg Lewis. *Fun facts: The Arsenal team featured cricketer Denis Compton who played alongside his brother Leslie / Liverpool dropped future manager Bob Paisley for the match even though he had scored against Merseyside rivals Everton in the semi-final.*

SNOOKER - WALTER DONALDSON

Walter Donaldson 51 - 46 Fred Davis

The 1950 World Snooker Championship was held at the Tower Circus in Blackpool between the 12th December 1949 and 18th March 1950. For the fourth year running the final was contested by Fred Davis and Walter Donaldson. Donaldson defeated Davis 51-46 to win his second and last world title. *Photo: Fred Davis (left) and Walter Donaldson in the 1948 Snooker World Championship final.*

GOLF - OPEN CHAMPIONSHIP - BOBBY LOCKE

The 1950 Open Championship was the 79th to be played and was held between the 5th and 7th July at Troon Golf Club in Troon, South Ayrshire, Scotland. Defending champion Bobby Locke of South Africa won the second of his four Open titles, two strokes ahead of runner-up Roberto De Vicenzo of Argentina. His total of 279 was a record for the Open Championship, beating the previous best of 283.

WIMBLEDON

Photo 1: Budge Patty with his men's singles trophy. Photo 2: Margaret du Pont (left) and Louise Brough collect the Women's Doubles Trophy.

Men's Singles Champion - Budge Patty - United States
Ladies Singles Champion - Louise Brough - United States

The 1950 Wimbledon Championships was the 64th staging of tournament and took place on the outdoor grass courts at the All England Lawn Tennis and Croquet Club in Wimbledon, London. It ran from the 26th June until the 8th July and was the third Grand Slam tennis event of 1950.

Men's Singles Final:

Country	Player	Set 1	Set 2	Set 3	Set 4
United States	Budge Patty	6	8	6	6
Australia	Frank Sedgman	1	10	2	3

Women's Singles Final:

Country	Player	Set 1	Set 2	Set 3
United States	Louise Brough	6	3	6
United States	Margaret duPont	1	6	1

Men's Doubles Final:

Country	Players	Set 1	Set 2	Set 3	Set 4	Set 5
Australia	John Bromwich / Adrian Quist	7	3	6	3	6
Australia	Geoff Brown / Bill Sidwell	5	6	3	6	2

Women's Doubles Final:

Country	Players	Set 1	Set 2	Set 3
United States	Louise Brough / Margaret duPont	6	5	6
United States	Shirley Fry / Doris Hart	4	7	1

Mixed Doubles Final:

Country	Players	Set 1	Set 2	Set 3
South Africa / United States	Eric Sturgess / Louise Brough	11	1	6
Australia / United States	Geoff Brown / Pat Todd	9	6	4

County Cricket

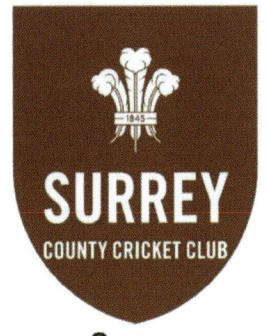

Lancashire

Surrey

1950 saw the 51st officially organised running of the County Championship. The Championship title was shared, for just the second time in its history, between Lancashire County Cricket Club and Surrey County Cricket Club.

Pos.	Team	Pld.	W	L	D	No Dec	Pts.
1	**Lancashire**	**28**	**16**	**2**	**10**	**0**	**220**
1	**Surrey**	**28**	**17**	**4**	**6**	**1**	**220**
3	Yorkshire	28	14	2	10	2	200
4	Warwickshire	28	8	6	13	1	132
5	Derbyshire	28	8	9	9	2	124

England vs West Indies - Test Series

The West Indies cricket team toured England and won the 1950 4-match Test series 3-1.
Fun fact: The second Test at Lord's was the first time that the West Indies had ever won a match in England.

1st Test | Old Trafford, 8th - 12th June - Result: England win by 202 runs

Innings	Team	Score	Overs	Team	Score	Overs
1st Innings	England	312	128.3	West Indies	215	93.5
2nd Innings	England	288	141.5	West Indies	183	81.2

2nd Test | Lord's, 24th - 29th June - Result: West Indies win by 326 runs

Innings	Team	Score	Overs	Team	Score	Overs
1st Innings	West Indies	326	131.2	England	151	106.4
2nd Innings	West Indies	425/6d	178	England	274	191.3

3rd Test | Trent Bridge, 20th - 25th July - Result: West Indies win by 10 wickets

Innings	Team	Score	Overs	Team	Score	Overs
1st Innings	England	223	98.4	West Indies	558	174.4
2nd Innings	England	436	245.2	West Indies	103/0	36.3

4th Test | The Oval, 12th - 16th August - Result: West Indies win by an innings and 56 runs

Innings	Team	Score	Overs	Team	Score	Overs
1st Innings	West Indies	503	194.2	England	344	179.4
2nd Innings	West Indies			England	103 f/o	69.3

THE COST OF LIVING

the pick-me-up that never lets you down!

SEAGERS EGG FLIP

Eggs and Wine - it'll do you a power of good!

COMPARISON CHART

	1950	1950 + Inflation	2019	% Change
3 Bedroom House	£2,400	£83,400	£236,676	+183.8%
Weekly Income	£4.14s.1d	£163.47	£569	+248.1%
Pint Of Beer	10d	£1.45	£3.69	+154.5%
Cheese (lb)	2s.2d	£3.76	£3.09	-17.8%
Bacon (lb)	2s.3d	£3.91	£2.65	-32.2%
The Beano	2d	29p	£2.75	+848.3%

New 1950 Rinso WITH SOLIUM
WASHES CLOTHES WHITER THAN NEW!
MAKES COLORS BRIGHTER THAN NEW!
NEW 1950 Rinso WITH SOLIUM PUTS SUNSHINE IN YOUR WASH!

SHOPPING

Brooke Bond Tea (¼lb)	10½d
Ovaltine (large tin)	4s
Lucozade (bottle)	2s.6d
Welgar Shredded Wheat	9d
Quaker Malted Corn Flakes (pkt.)	8d
Robertson's Golliberry Jelly Preserve (1lb)	1s.5½d
Ryvita (packet)	1s
Rowntree's Fruit Gums	2½d
Mars Bar (large)	5d
Amami Wave Set	2s.6½d
Arrid Underarm Cream Deodorant (jar)	2s.5d
Phillips' Dental Magnesia Toothpaste	1s.4d
Brylshave	1s.9d
Blue Gillette Razor Blades (10)	3s.4d
Eno's Fruit Salt (regular size)	2s.3d
Famel Family Cough Syrup	2s.6d
Glymiel Jelly (small tube)	1s.4d
Beecham's Powders (2)	5½d
Andrews Liver Salt (4oz tin)	1s.3d
Crookes Halibut Oil (100)	3s.6d
Woodward's Gripe Water	1s.9d
Fab Washing Powder	11d
Lux - Double Size	1s.3d
Lifeguard Disinfectant	1s
Wiles Vitamin Dog Food (can)	10d

Whatever the pleasure *Player's* complete it

PLAYER'S NAVY CUT CIGARETTES · MEDIUM OR MILD · PLAIN OR CORK TIPPED
[NCC 704ff]

It takes **Quix** to show you the <u>new</u> way to brighter WASHING-UP!

JUST A LITTLE **Quix** KILLS GREASE COMPLETELY— LEAVES DISHES AND GLASSWARE **SPARKLING**!

Quix SUDS ARE GENTLE—TAKE THAT WASHING-UP LOOK OFF YOUR HANDS TOO!

60 BOWLS OF RICH SUDS IN EVERY LARGE BOTTLE!

BETTER THAN **ANYTHING** ELSE FOR WASHING-UP!

REAL VALUE AT 1/6^D

Quix CONCENTRATED SUDS

Dad loves Mackintosh's

Ever since he was a boy he's had a soft spot for Mackintosh's, and he'd still polish them off like any youngster—if Mum wasn't looking!

Dave loves Mackintosh's

You can't keep that boy away from them! A bagful simply goes nowhere with Dave. "Smashing chocolates!" he says. "Smashing toffees!"

...to-day everybody's favourite is

Mackintosh's Quality Street

JOHN MACKINTOSH & SONS LIMITED, HALIFAX

It's time you had a BSA

Admire its rich ruby colour
Inhale its exquisite bouquet
Relish the really excellent flavour of

GILBEY'S PORT

YOU'LL BE GLAD YOU GOT GILBEY'S

CLOTHES

My Lady — CORSETS AND BRASSIÈRES

...the foundation for fashion's circle

Chosen by women since 1884 for their comfortable control. To be in tune with fashion, make sure your foundation garments are "My Lady."

WATERHOUSE REYNOLDS & CO. LTD., LEICESTER

Women's Clothing

C&A Winter Topcoat	£3.19s.11d
Plastic Mac	9s.11d
Richard Shops Full Skirted Frock	£5.6s
Barker's Grey Rayon Striped Dress	£2.9s.11d
Cotton Pinarette - Housewives' Overall	15s.6d
Fine Ribbed Luxury Jumper	6s
12 Panel Swing Skirt	£1.5s
Ambrose Wilson Corset	19s.3d
Kayser Bondor Stockings	7s.1d
Platform Shoes - Gaberdine Uppers	£1
Lilley & Skinner Jungle Sandals	£1.9s.4d

Men's Clothing

RAF Greatcoat	£1.9s.6d
Fleecy Coat Lining	12s.11d
Australian Woollen Grey Shirt	19s.9d
Tootal Tie	3s
Officers Brown Leather Boots	£1.4s.6d

OTHER PRICES

MG Midget Car	£569.7s.3d
Ford Anglia Car	£310
RGD 12in TV	£109.11s.1d
Rent A Radio - Radio Rentals (per week)	from 2s.6d
Dudley Vacuum Cleaner	£11.14s
Hoover Vacuum Cleaner (rebuilt)	£5.15s
Accurist Precision Watch	from £5.19s
Swan Pen	£1.10s.7d
Goya Great Expectations Perfume	£3
Mighty Midget Toy Electric Racer	£1.2s.6d
Seagers Egg Flip (bottle)	17s
Stones Original Ginger Wine	7s
VP Wine (½ bottle)	3s.3d
Embassy Cigarettes (20)	3s.6d
Woman's Weekly Magazine	3d

Introducing the NEW RGD MODEL 1700

This new R.G.D. Television receiver employs a 12-in. flat-ended tube and 10-in. speaker. Combining the traditional R.G.D. qualities of technical excellence and a beautiful cabinet, this model is now available at £109 11s. 1d. including purchase tax.

Your local R.G.D. retailer will be pleased to arrange a demonstration.

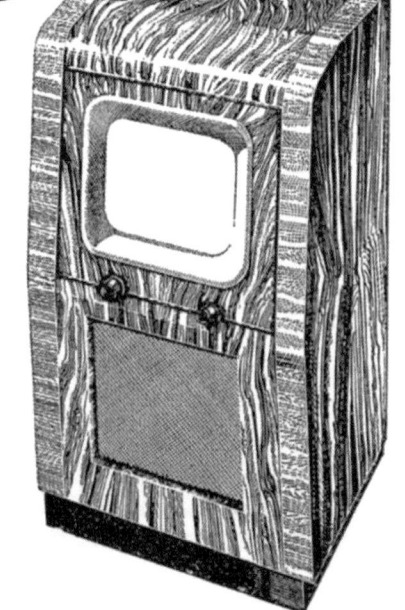

The Aristocrat of Radio and Television

RADIO GRAMOPHONE DEVELOPMENT COMPANY LIMITED
BRIDGNORTH   SHROPSHIRE

Money Conversion Table

	1950 'Old Money'		Value Today
Farthing	¼d	0.1p	3½p
Half Penny	½d	0.21p	7p
Penny	1d	0.42p	14p
Threepence	3d	1.25p	43p
Sixpence	6d	2.5p	87p
Shilling	1s	5p	£1.74
Florin	2s	10p	£3.47
Half Crown	2s.6d	12.5p	£4.34
Crown	5s	25p	£8.69
Ten Shillings	10s	50p	£17.37
Pound	20s	£1	£34.75
Guinea	21s	£1.05	£36.49
Five Pounds	£5	£5	£173.75
Ten Pounds	£10	£10	£347.50

The Friendly Link...

A happy purpose is served by Capstan in providing a pleasant link of friendship in any company. This really good cigarette is *made to make friends.*

Have a CAPSTAN

CAPSTAN Navy Cut CIGARETTES
MEDIUM STRENGTH
W.D. & H.O. WILLS, BRISTOL & LONDON.

Teach your son safe shooting

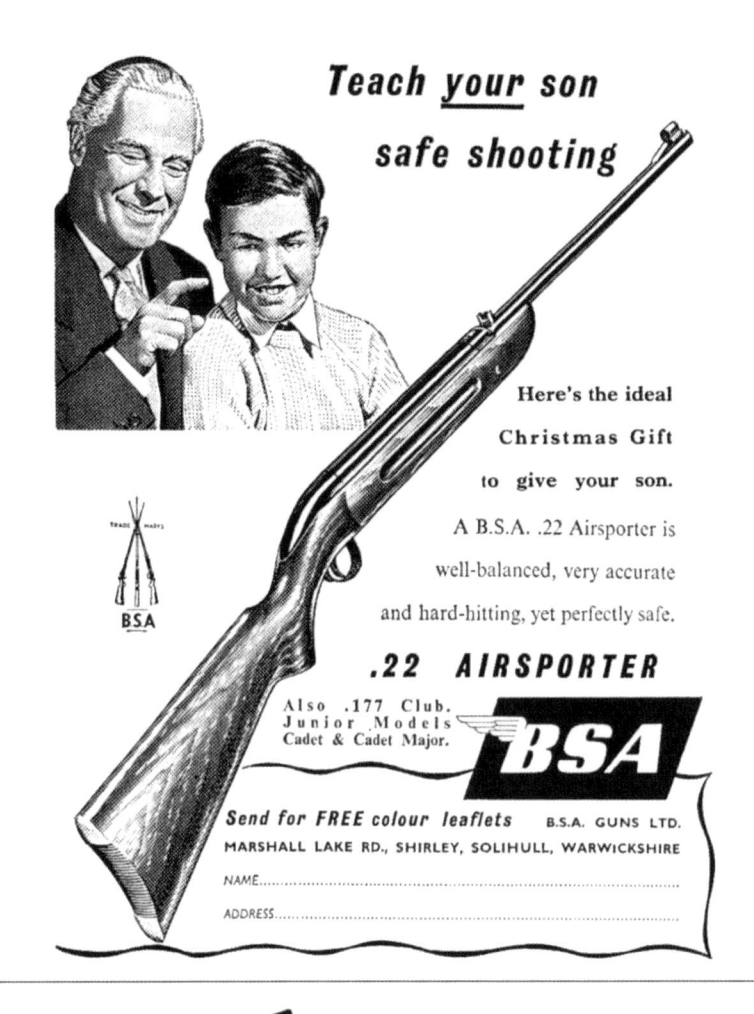

Here's the ideal Christmas Gift to give your son. A B.S.A. .22 Airsporter is well-balanced, very accurate and hard-hitting, yet perfectly safe.

.22 AIRSPORTER

Also .177 Club. Junior Models Cadet & Cadet Major.

BSA

Send for FREE colour leaflets B.S.A. GUNS LTD.
MARSHALL LAKE RD., SHIRLEY, SOLIHULL, WARWICKSHIRE

NAME..................
ADDRESS..................

THE NEW T.D. MIDGET WITH THE *plus* FEATURES

The new T.D. Midget incorporates many important *plus* features and reaches a new high standard of comfort and roadworthiness. Here is a car with all the liveliness and distinctive character of its famous predecessors. A car with a mission ... to uphold and further the MG tradition of Safety Fast!

plus coil spring independent front-wheel suspension. The new Midget rides smoothly — hugs the road at high speeds. Bumps and pot-holes are ironed out.

plus extra body-width for greater comfort, combined with sturdier general construction. This new model is tougher, more rugged than its predecessors.

plus Luvax Girling hydraulic piston-type shock absorbers. Enable car to cruise comfortably maintaining high average speeds over short and long journeys.

plus newly designed Lockheed hydraulic brakes on all four wheels. Even more powerful braking is part of the MG tradition of Safety Fast.

plus the latest direct-acting rack-and-pinion type steering. This gives an unusually light yet positive touch which is entirely free from vibration.

£445.0.0 EX WORKS PLUS
£124.7.3 PURCHASE TAX

MG

Safety Fast!

THE MG CAR COMPANY LIMITED, SALES DIVISION, COWLEY, OXFORD
Overseas Business: Nuffield Exports Ltd., Oxford and 41 Piccadilly, London, W.1
London Showrooms: University Motors Ltd., 7, Hertford Street, W.1.

Printed in Great Britain
by Amazon